Available from:
Christian International Ministries
P.O. Box 9000
Santa Rosa Beach, FL 32459
1-800-388-5308

Printed in the USA

PROPHETIC MINISTRY BY FAITH

Ministering Spiritual Gifts Series
Student Workbook
Part 3

TABLE OF CONTENTS

Introduction

Prophetic Principles

Prophetic Ministry by Faith 1

Accurate/Inaccurate Prophesies, Part 1 14

Accurate/Inaccurate Prophesies, Part 2 19

Prophetic Pitfalls

The Prophet Elijah Pitfall of Discouragement and Pity 30

The Prophet Moses' Pitfall of Overprotectiveness 36

Prophet Jonah's Pride and Judgment Pitfall 40

Prophet Balaam's Pitfall: True Prophesier but False Prophet 45

Activations

Activations Overview 54

Activation Guidelines 56

INTRODUCTION

This workbook includes the following segments: prophetic principles, which are helpful in giving practical advice and answering common questions from the standpoint of the person prophesying; prophetic pitfalls which describes snares that can hinder ministers; and activations, which will give you the opportunity to minister spiritual gifts in a safe environment.

PROPHETIC PRINCIPLES

Student: The Prophetic Principles segment of this manual is intended to 1) infuse you with faith to believe that you can prophesy; 2)) provide you with principles and practical advice as a prophetic minister and one who is exposed to prophetic ministry; 3) present you with proper principles for ministering personal prophecy.

Prophetic Ministry by Faith 1

Accurate/Inaccurate Prophesies, Part 1 14

Accurate/Inaccurate Prophesies, Part 2 19

PROPHETIC MINISTRY BY FAITH

Romans 12:5
He that prophesies, let him prophesy according to the proportion of his faith.

I. IS THE PROPHET DIVINELY GIFTED TO MINISTER PROPHETICALLY TO ANY WHO COME BEFORE HIM?

Review:
Does God like/desire to talk to His people?
Yes. He is a personal God who desires intimate fellowship. When sin entered the human race, our ears were dulled and we lost our desire and sensitivity to God's voice. Under our new covenant, Jesus spoke, "My sheep hear my voice."
Can you set a time and place to prophesy?
Yes. The believer does not have to wait on the Holy Spirit's unction, but by an act of the human will/ we can stir up and activate the gifts. (See 2 Timothy 1:6)
Can you "make" God talk?
God is always trying to communicate. We don't all hear his voice on the same "frequency." We must cooperate with him; not make Him talk.

II. THE PRINCIPLE OF SPIRITUAL GIFT STEWARDSHIP

A. FAITH APPROPRIATION

1) Every move of God takes the occasional supernatural experiences of a few and appropriates it for the many. It takes a "special and unique" thing and makes it normal.

____

____

2) There were people prophesying before the Prophetic Movement, but they were unique. Not many were prophesying. There were people speaking in tongues before the Pentecostal Movement, but the Pentecostal Movement made it an open revelation for everyone.

3) The Prophetic Movement brought forth the principle of **spiritual** gift stewardship.

B. PROPORTION OF FAITH
Romans 12:6, *"He that prophesies, let him prophesy according to the proportion of his faith."*

1) Some have more faith to prophesy than others.

2) Some have faith for specific areas.

3) If you are gifted prophetically, it should be part of your lifestyle, not just on special occasions or circumstances.

____
____
____
____
____

C. BELIEVE
Mark 11:23, 24; *"Whatsoever things you desire, when you pray, believe you have received them and you will have them."*

You get what you put your faith out for!

D. STEWARDSHIP
1 Peter 4:10 *"As every man has received the gift, even so minister the same one to another, as good stewards of the manifold grace of God."*

1) *Steward* – a man entrusted with the **management** of the household or **estate** of another.

2) *Stewardship* means **managing** the assets and making them profitable.

I CORINTHIANS 12:7
"The manifestation of the spirit is given to us."

E. *SPIRIT* OF PROPHET SUBJECT TO THE PROPHET
Corinthians 14:32 *"The spirit of the prophet is subject to the prophet."*

1) *Subject* means: "to subordinate, to rank under."

2) If the spirit of the prophet is subject to the prophet for the purpose of restraint, it must also be true that it is subject for the purpose of **activation**. The spirit of the prophet is **responsible** to obey the prophet.

3) The context of this verse is that the people were prophesying too much, and all prophesying at the same time. If everyone starts prophesying at the same time, then you need restraint.

____.

F. STIR UP THE GIFTS
II Timothy 1:6 *"Stir up the gift that is in you by the laying on of my hands."*

1) *Stir* means: to "**fan into a flame**."

2) Analogy: If the campfire is getting low, stirring it will cause the flames to come back up.

____

____.

G. STIRRING UP THE GIFT OF GOD

ELISHA
In II Kings 3:10-16, Elisha prophesied to Johoram and Jehoshaphat. Jehoshaphat had made an alliance with Johoram (the son of Ahab and Jezebel), and with the king of Moab (an ungodly king).

1) (v. 11) *"Who poured water on the hands of Elijah."*
This helps give credibility to Elisha as a prophet.

2) (v. 14) Elisha didn't feel like prophesying to Jehoram. He's emotional, and realizes this is not the best way to give a prophetic word.

3) (v. 15) "Bring me a minstrel." Even in the Old Testament, Elisha had to stir up the gift.

JESUS
In John 4:6, Jesus, weary from His journey, stirred up the gift and ministered to the woman at the well. He was tired, thirsty, and hungry. He stirred Himself up to minister to the woman at the well. The result—the whole town was transformed.

1) (vs. 7-9) Jesus addressed and broke down racial barriers erected by men.

2) (v. 39) "And many Samaritans of that city believed on Him because of the saying of the woman, (who) testified, 'He told me all that I ever did'."

3) Prophetic evangelism—we must be prepared to stir up and use the gifts in various settings.

III. WISDOM IN DISCHARGING PROPHETIC MINISTRY

Q: For those who are activated, is it now wisdom and divine order to minister to everybody they come in contact with?

A: We should be in a place that when God calls on us, we are ready to minister. On the other hand, we shouldn't always respond. Maintain balance.

IV. WHAT ARE THE DIFFERENT LEVELS OF GIFTING AND ANOINTING IN THE PROPHETIC REALM? ARE ALL WHO PROPHESY CONSIDERED PROPHETS?

- In I Corinthians 12:28, Paul asks rhetorically if all are prophets. The answer is clearly no. Yet he states in I Corinthians 14:39 that we are to covet to prophesy, and in verse 31 that we may all prophesy one by one.

- Individuals may flow in the **spirit** of **prophecy** which comes upon a congregation, or in the **gift** of **prophecy**, which is given by the Holy Spirit to certain believers. This does not mean they are prophets.

  ⇨ Saul, who was tormented by an evil spirit, prophesied when he got around the prophets (I Samuel 19:24).

A. PROPHETS

1) Are one of the five-fold ministers of Christ who hold governmental authority in the Church, not just individuals who prophesy. In fact, prophesying may make up a small portion of certain prophet's ministries.

2) They may also be gifted to teach, shepherd, administrate, etc. For example, Isaiah was a consultant to kings and governments; Joseph administered a worldwide food distribution program; and David ruled all of Israel, and he also had an anointed music ministry.

3) The prophet's ministry cannot be limited to just prophesying.

B. LEVELS OF AUTHORITY

1) Even among the prophets there is a difference in levels of authority. Those who have years of seasoned and proven ministries and who have been through God's process of maturity and testing will have more authoritative prophetic pronouncements than the "sons of the prophets" who are new in ministry.

2) Elijah moved in great authority by shutting up the heavens and calling down fire, etc. Yet concurrently in Israel there were at least one hundred other prophets which Obadiah, Ahab's governor, hid in caves to protect from God's wrath (I Kings 18:4).

3) Samuel was a key prophetic leader in Israel's history whose words never fell to the ground. Because of his stature and maturity, he was the overseer of an entire company of prophets (I Samuel 19:20).

4) God is raising up elders in the prophetic ministry who can be fathers and mothers to birth and train many in this restoration move of the Holy Spirit. These will be mature men and women in ministry who can help us avoid the **excesses** and **imbalances**. They will stress **characters** as well as **giftings** and will stress **seeking God's face** as well as His hand of favor.

V. HOW SHOULD A PERSON PROPERLY RESPOND TO PERSONAL PROPHESY?

- Prophesy is **conditional** and its fulfillment requires **obedience** and **faithfulness**. God's "I will's" expressed to the children of Israel concerning taking them into the promised land, worked for only two men out of 600,000 (Exodus 6:6-8; Numbers 13:26-33, Jeremiah 18:8-10).

- After prophecy is recorded, write it out and meditate upon the prophecy.

- We must have the prophecy in front of us if we are to wage a good warfare with it (I Timothy 1:18).

- Elders and overseers should be allowed to evaluate the prophecies their people receive.

- Prophecies should be reviewed to determine the following:

  1) *What (if any) action is prescribed?*
  When Jehu was anointed king, he immediately acted on the prophecy and killed Jezebel and the sons of Ahab (II Kings 9 & 10).

  2) *What attitudes, character traits, and mindsets need to be adjusted?*
  Joseph's attitude was adjusted during Mary's pregnancy (Matthew 1:20-25).

  3) *What must simply be left for God to fulfill in His way and timing?*
  One example is the prophecy to Mary about bearing Christ (Luke 1:31-36).

- Realize that one prophetic utterance may have a varied a **timetable** of fulfillment. Mary received a prophetic word from the angel Gabriel concerning the birth of Christ which had an extremely varied time table for fulfillment, even though it was only three sentences long (Luke 1:31-33).

Thou shalt conceive in thy womb"
(Happened almost immediately)
"and shalt bring forth a son"
(Came to pass about 9 months later)
"He shall be great, and shall be called the Son of the Highest."
(Came to pass partially upon Jesus' triumphal entry into Jerusalem, Luke 19:38)
"And he shall reign over the house of Jacob forever, and of his kingdom there shall be no end."
(Still coming to pass)

⇨ **Note**: for more in depth teaching on these subjects, see Chapters 13, 14, 16, 17 and 18 in *Prophets and Personal Prophecy,* by Dr. Bill Hamon.

VI. WILL THE PERSON RECEIVING THE PROPHETIC WORD ALWAYS HAVE A WITNESS IN THEIR SPIRIT THAT IT IS ACCURATE AND FROM GOD?

A. ROMANS 8:16

The **witness** of the Spirit is one way to determine that prophetic utterance is from the Lord. *"The Spirit itself beareth witness with our spirit, that we are children of God."* (Romans 8:16)

1) It is probably the most subjective way of determining true prophecy, since our "witness" can be clouded by human **mindsets**, incorrect knowledge, and by not **knowing** our own heart.

2) Jeremiah said the heart is wicked and deceitful above all things, who can know it? (Jeremiah 17:9).

3) Therefore, we should not discard a word as inaccurate or incorrect simply because we do not witness to it.

B. II KINGS 8:7-13
Elisha looked at Hazael and wept, then prophesied that Hazael would kill the people of Israel, burn their cities, kill the young men, dash their babies against the rocks, and rip open their pregnant women.

1) Hazael responded by asking "Am I a dog? I would never do that sort of thing." He didn't feel he was capable of such degradation; it wasn't in his heart.

2) When Elisha prophesied that Hazael would be the next king of Syria, he suffocated Ben-hadad, king of Syria, and became king in his place. He then continually conquered and oppressed Israel throughout his reign as the Syrian king.

3) Murder was in his heart when Elisha prophesied to him, but he did not recognize it and felt he was incapable of such action.

VII. DOES GOD ALLOW FALSE PROPHECIES? IF SO, THEN WHY?

A. DEUTERONOMY 13:1-3
To prove the **heart** of God's people. Will they follow God or some miracle worker who draws them away from His commandments and will?

B. I CORINTHIANS 11:19
"For there must be also heresies among you, that they which are approved may be made manifest among you." The contrast between **true** and **false** provides an opportunity to compare and contrast the two and to **highlight** the true.

C. ROMANS 1:28
To provide **delusion** and **deception** to the dishonest.

D. JEREMIAH 23
To bring judgment upon the **disobedient** and to separate the **curious** from the committed. The controversy swirling around the prophetic will increase greatly in the days to come, because God never makes it easy to come into present truth. Like Gideon's 32,000 men, all those who are afraid of imbalance, extremes, and error will have opportunity to go home.

VIII. WHAT ABOUT PROPHECIES WHICH SEEM CONTRADICTORY?

- We can see from looking at prophecies concerning Jesus in Scripture that it would be easy to be confused and feel that the prophecies concerning the Messiah were contradictory and mutually exclusive. For instance, it was prophesied that:

  ⇨ The Messiah would be born in Bethlehem (Micah 5:2)

  ⇨ His light would shine in Galilee Isaiah (9:1, 2)

  ⇨ God's Son would come out of Egypt (Hosea 11:1)

- In fact, these prophecies confused the people who saw the miracles of Jesus, but who insisted He could not be the Christ because they did not know of His birth in Bethlehem. (John 7:42)

- **Incomplete** or **improper** knowledge will cause people to reject a true prophetic word. Prophecies which seem **contradictory** today will normally all prove to be **true** as God works things out in His timing.

IX. WILL A PERSONAL PROPHECY REVEAL ALL OF GOD'S WILL FOR MY ENTIRE LIFE?

- Personal prophecy should not be accepted as limiting or as being the all-inclusive will of God for an individual's life and ministry, but only as one piece of the puzzle.

- Abraham had 11 personal prophecies which were ever expanding God's purpose for His life and giving greater clarity to his call and purpose.

- I Corinthians 13:8—Paul said "we prophesy in part."

___

___

___

⇨ **Note**: See *Prophets and Personal Prophecy*, Chapter 13.

X. IS THERE A NORMAL COURSE OF TIME FOR A PROPHECY TO BE FULFILLED?

- The word of the Lord is normally spoken of in the context of a person's lifetime and even their heritage (generations). It is rare for a prophecy about a person's ultimate call and ministry to be fulfilled in weeks, months, or even years.

    - Samuel 16:13—David was anointed for kingship while still a youth, but he did not come to the throne until the age of 30.

____

____

____

____

____

XI. DOES PROPHECY NORMALLY COME TO PASS IN THE WAY MAN ENVISIONS?

A. SPIRIT OF REVELATION

Christ was the fulfillment of hundreds of Old Testament prophecies, yet men in their natural understanding of Scripture could not receive him as the Messiah (John 6:41; 10:24).

B. HISTORICAL EVENT

Peter spoke by revelation in Acts 2:16 when he said, *"This is that spoken of by the Prophet Joel"* concerning the outpouring of the Holy Spirit. Those without revelation asked, "What meaneth this?" while others mocked (v. 12, 13). This was a historical event without precedent which fulfilled prophecy, yet many did not perceive its importance and therefore missed out on its benefits.

C. JUDGMENT

Paul took a scripture from Isaiah 28, in which Isaiah prophesied judgment upon Israel via the Babylonian invasion and their foreign language, and applied it to mean we should speak in tongues today. Though seemingly out of context and hermeneutically incorrect, modern theologians must accept this as valid since Paul used it in this context in I Corinthians 14:21.

ADDITIONAL NOTES

ACCURATE/INACCURATE PROPHECIES

I. IS THE OLD TESTAMENT STANDARD FOR TRUE & FALSE PROPHETS APPLICABLE FOR NEW TESTAMENT PROPHETIC MINISTRY?

- In the Old Testament, one sin cast Adam and Eve out of the Garden; one mistake kept Moses out of Canaan; one sin cast Lucifer out of heaven; and one mistake caused a man to be a false prophet, according to Deuteronomy 18.

- While priests functioned as representatives of man to God via sacrifices and ministrations, the prophets represented God to man with their divine judgments and decrees. Therefore, the Old Testament prophet was required to speak the very word of the Lord each time he opened his mouth, and could not afford to speak falsely or presumptuously lest he lead the entire nation into error.

- In the New Testament, Jesus Christ is our mediator (not the prophet, nor our pastor), and we have the complete Scriptures to rely on. This does not do away with the need for prophets and prophecy, but it does place them in a less dutiful position, (under the grace of the New Testament), than their Old Testament Counterparts.

- In the Old Testament, the key was whether the **prophet** was leading people to or away from **God**. The standard was if it doesn't come to **pass**, the prophet speaks in the name of **another** God, or says **something** God did not tell him to say, the **prophet** will then die. In the New Testament, the standard is based on on the person's **heart** motive and **character** (Jude 11; 2 Peter 2:15). Because we can approach God personally, the standard of judging the accuracy of the word is now on the **hearer**.

II. PROPER STANDARDS FOR PROPHETS

- The standard for true/false prophets is only partially based upon their ministry and **accurate** words.. Credence must be given to other areas of life, such as Messianic prophecy in the book of Numbers (24:17-19), yet his character and lifestyle were that of a false prophet (II Peter 2:15; Jude 11-13).

- The following scriptures illustrate the understanding that present day prophetic ministry is from the Lord, but via fallible people:

    - I Corinthians 14:29 *"Let the prophets speak two or three, and let the others judge."*

    - I Thessalonians 5:20-21 *"Despise not prophesying. Test all things; hold fast that which is good".* *Test* means to prove the value or worth of something, such as in metallurgy; to test metal, how pure it is.
    - II Corinthians 4:7 *"But we have this treasure in earthen vessels, that the excellency of the power may be of God, and not of us."*

    - I Corinthians 13:12 *"We see through a glass darkly."*

    - I Corinthians 13:9 *"We know in part, and we prophesy in part."*

III. THE DILEMMA FOR ALL THOSE WHO WOULD PROPHESY

- The dilemma is that you have to be fallible, but never show it. Those who operate in the prophetic ministry are often placed in a precarious position which creates a real dilemma. If they present themselves as infallible and contend they never "miss it," they become heretical because Biblical doctrine clearly presents the fact that God alone is infallible, on the basis of each individual being an earthen vessel and seeing through a glass darkly, and is susceptible to error and mistakes. This seemingly high standard for prophetic ministry (which is actually motivated by a legalistic, Pharisaical spirit) leads to deception and eventually cultic error and control.

- If the prophet proves his fallibility by making a mistake and speaking a word which does not come to pass, then he stands accused by a certain segment of the church. This segment, either through ignorance or guile and resentment, eagerly waits for the chance to make accusations of "false prophet."

- Perhaps this dilemma is one way God has to ensure His prophets do not become puffed up with pride in their gifting or revelation. There is constant realization that they are a "heartbeat from humility" and must be totally reliant on the grace of God.

____

____

____

____

____

IV. ACCOUNTABILITY FOR ALL MINISTRIES

A. Regarding false/inaccurate prophecies, undue emphasis can be placed upon the prophetic ministry to prove itself 100% accurate. The necessity of other five-fold ministries being accountable for their words and actions is not being taken into account.

1) While it is true that "thus saith the Lord" demands a greater accountability due to the authority claimed in the utterance, this does not do away with the need for accountability for a teacher's teaching or a pastor's counsel. James notes particularly that teachers will be held to a higher standard of accountability (James 3:1).

2) Typically, more emphasis is placed upon the prophetic ministry than other five-fold ministry offices or functions.

B. While promoting accountability for prophetic ministries, certain ones will develop a "witch hunt" mentality against the prophetic.

C. This is not the Biblical pattern of accountability, and will only cause the investigators to be in jeopardy of having each and every one of their sins and failures exposed for the whole world to see.

V. STATEMENTS AND QUESTIONS FOR CONSIDERATION

- If one holds to the premise that prophets must be 100% accurate, then how are prophets to be trained?

- Is it possible to train and develop the giftings and abilities of our redeemed human spirit in the same way we can train and develop our natural giftings and abilities?

- If we hold to the premise that mature prophets are always accurate and never fail in perfectly declaring the mind and will of God, then the ultimate conclusion of this "infallibility" would require their followers to place their prophetic declarations on the same level of authority and revelation as the Scriptures. What are the results of such perception?

ADDITIONAL NOTES

ACCURATE/INACCURATE PROPHECIES

I. A DEFINITION OF TERMS IS NECESSARY IN DISCUSSING INACCURATE PROPHECIES

A. FALSE VS. INACCURATE

Because the definition of "false" has the connotation of being deceitful, lying, or having a wrong motive, it may be better to call prophecies which do not come to pass, or are incorrect in detail, "inaccurate." "False" is a label which, when put on a minister, calls into question lifestyle, doctrine, integrity, and spirit. "Inaccurate" only brings into question the specific accuracy of particular prophetic utterances, not the minister himself.

B. DEFINITIONS

1) *False*: not true; incorrect; wrong; untruthful; lying; unfaithful; not real. (From a Latin word "fallere", meaning deceive.) **False** has to do with the prophet, not the prophecy. It has to do with the *person,* not the **performance**.

2) *Inaccurate*: not accurate; not exact or correct; not according to truth; erroneous.

3) *Presumptuous*: literal definition "taking something for granted." For our discussion, we will define it as a prophecy which is spoken from one's **own spirit** (mind, will, opinion, conviction, doctrine, etc.) rather than from the **Holy Spirit**, but without evil intent.

4) *Accurate*: You **said** what God told you to **say**.

II. SEEMINGLY INACCURATE PROPHECIES

When dealing with inaccurate prophecies, it is extremely important to substantiate the inaccuracy before making a judgment that a prophecy is truly wrong.

There are some prophecies which may seem inaccurate at the time given, but which prove to be true when proven out by time and the person's experience.

Listed below are several Biblical examples of prophecies which could have seemed inaccurate, but which were proven to be true:

A. JESUS' PROPHECY ABOUT LAZARUS, JOHN 11:4

> *"This sickness is not unto death, but for the glory of God, that the Son of God might be glorified thereby."* The NIV states more specifically: *"This sickness will not end in death."*

"This sickness is not unto death"; to us means that Lazarus won't die. This prophecy was misunderstood by Jesus' disciples, who had to be told plainly "Lazarus is dead" (v. 14). For about four days, this prophecy was inaccurate according to our standards.

____
____
____
____

B. JONAH'S PROPHECY OF JUDGMENT TO NINEVEH

This is another example of a **conditional** word which was changed by **repentance**. Jonah put no conditions on it, yet **God** changed his mind and stayed **judgment** because of their **repentance**. This word was **accurate** because Jonah told them what God told him to say.

C. ISAIAH'S PROPHECY TO HEZEKIAH, ISAIAH 38

The first prophecy stated that Hezekiah would die from the serious illness he was battling. But Hezekiah's cries of repentance caused God to change His mind and He sent Isaiah back to the King with a new word of extended life. The second word was emphatic, with an accompanying sign given of the sun going back 10 degrees. *These types of words, if given in a public setting or shared extensively with others, can cause those who don't know about the follow-up to feel they are false prophecies.*

D. PERSONAL EXAMPLES OF A SEEMINGLY INACCURATE PROPHECY

I was ministering to a woman about a nest egg of money she had, and that God was going to give her wisdom how to invest it. The pastor felt it was a wrong word, since he knew the woman well and knew she had no extra money, but lived paycheck to paycheck. However, on checking with her after the prophecy he found she had just received an unexpected insurance settlement which was quite substantial and the word applied perfectly.

III. POSSIBLE PRESUMPTUOUS PROPHECIES

A. NATHAN'S PRONOUNCEMENT TO DAVID TO BUILD GOD A TEMPLE

> I Chronicles 17:1-4 *"Now it came to pass, as David sat in his house, that David said to Nathan the prophet, Lo, I dwell in a house of cedars, but the ark of the covenant of the Lord remaineth under curtains. Then Nathan said unto David, Do all that is in thine heart; for God is with thee. And it came to pass the same night, that the word of God came to Nathan, saying, Go and tell David my servant, Thus saith the Lord, Thou shalt not build me a house to dwell in."*

Even though Nathan does not prophesy in v. 2, the emphasis in v. 1 is on "Nathan the prophet." Nathan spoke to David from his position as prophet, just as David spoke to Nathan from his position as king. Though Nathan did not preface his remarks with "thus saith the Lord," he does attribute the building of a temple to be God's will for David. We could call this a *presumptuous word* given out of Nathan's own spirit.

It became obvious upon Nathan's word to David not to build the temple that the first word was incorrect and should therefore be disregarded. The Bible does not mention that Nathan apologized or in any way acknowledged to David and the leadership of Israel that his initial word was in error. Evidently it was unnecessary, and did not affect Nathan's reputation as a prophet of God.

This is made evident when, at a later time in David's life, Nathan confronted him with his sin of adultery and murder. Because Nathan had "missed it" once before, David could have become defensive and critical of Nathan's prophetic ministry, thereby excusing his sin. However, David quickly received Nathan's rebuke, indicating that Nathan's prophetic authority was not diminished by his one recorded mistake. Nathan was sent by God with divine authority and approval, and ministered correction to David as the mouthpiece of God.

____

____

____

____

____

____

B. DISCIPLES AT TYRE PROPHESIED TO PAUL, ACTS 21:4

> *"And finding disciples, we tarried there seven days; who said to Paul through the Spirit that he should not go up to Jerusalem."*

This appears to be This appears to be correct **revelation** but the wrong **application** and **interpretation**.

Paul previously stated that he went *"bound in the Spirit unto Jerusalem,"* and that he *"proposed in the spirit. . .to go to Jerusalem."* (Acts 19:21; 20:22) In his letter to the Romans, Paul specifically asked for *"prayer from them that do not believe in Judea; and that my service (offerings) which I have for Jerusalem may be accepted of the saints,"* (Romans 15:31).

Paul was traveling from Asia back to Jerusalem on this final missionary journey, solely for the purpose of taking a large offering from the other churches to the Jewish believers (Acts 24:17; Romans 15:27). He surely could have sent this money by another hand, particularly after being warned repeatedly of the dangers waiting in Jerusalem. However, it was not only the money, but the fact that the money came from the predominantly Gentile believers which Paul ministered to. This showed the Jewish leaders (in a tangible way) the gratitude of the Gentile believers toward those from whom the gospel had originated and sprung. Paul was not only bringing financial assistance, he was declaring unity among continually misunderstood factions of Jewish and Gentile believers which plagued the early Church. This type of self-sacrifice is a mark of true fatherhood in the Body of Christ.

____
____
____
____
____
____

IV. POSSIBLE INACCURATE PROPHECY

AGABUS' PROPHECY TO PAUL, ACTS 21

> 11 *"So shall the Jews in Jerusalem bind the man who owns this girdle, and shall deliver him into the hands of the Gentiles."*

1) At the heart of this prophecy are the two particular details of "binding" and "delivering," neither of which appears to be fulfilled literally according to the Biblical narrative.

a) Greek word for bind *"deo"* means "to bind, be in bonds, knit, tie, bind."

b) Greek word for deliver is *"paradidomi"* means "to surrender, yield up, entrust, transmit."

____
____
____

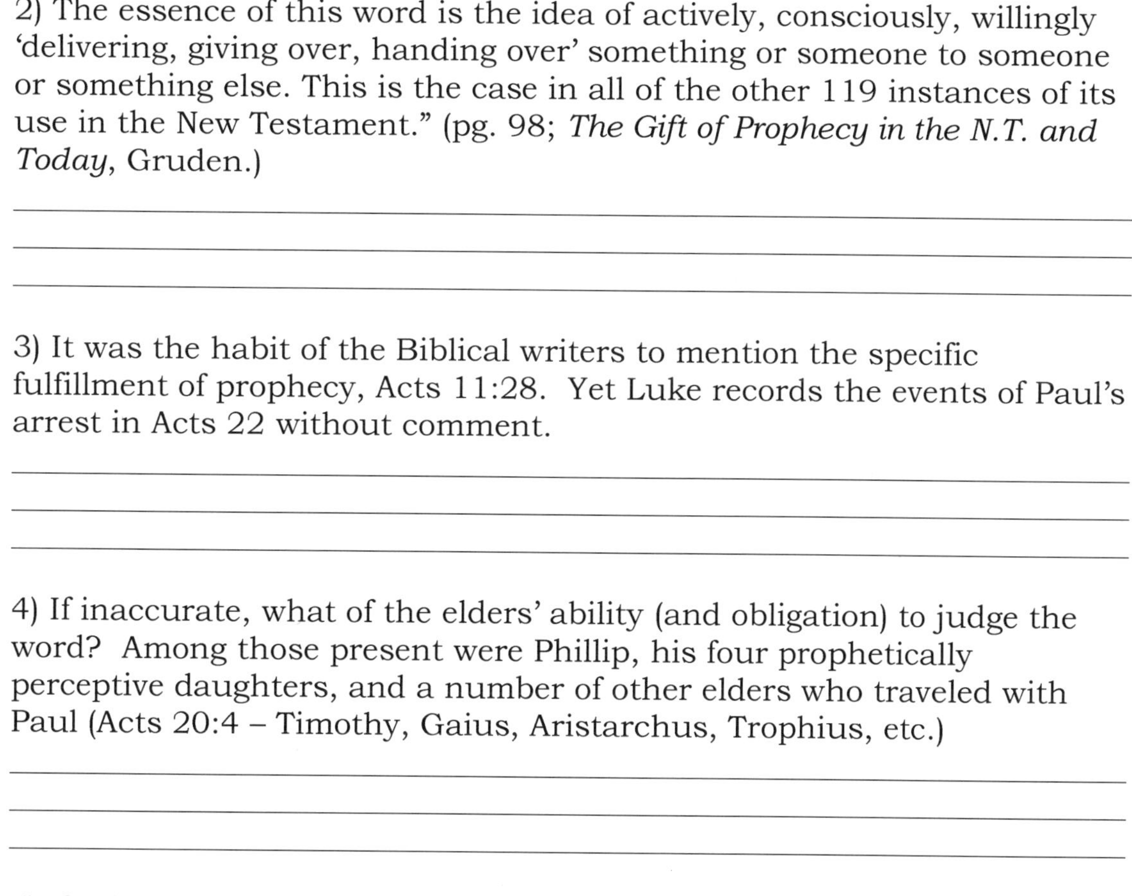

2) The essence of this word is the idea of actively, consciously, willingly 'delivering, giving over, handing over' something or someone to someone or something else. This is the case in all of the other 119 instances of its use in the New Testament." (pg. 98; *The Gift of Prophecy in the N.T. and Today*, Gruden.)

3) It was the habit of the Biblical writers to mention the specific fulfillment of prophecy, Acts 11:28. Yet Luke records the events of Paul's arrest in Acts 22 without comment.

4) If inaccurate, what of the elders' ability (and obligation) to judge the word? Among those present were Phillip, his four prophetically perceptive daughters, and a number of other elders who traveled with Paul (Acts 20:4 – Timothy, Gaius, Aristarchus, Trophius, etc.)

5) If this prophecy is inaccurate, how do we interpret Acts 28:17? This Scripture seems to contrast directly with Acts 23:27.

a) Paul agreed with Agabus that he was "delivered" to the Romans.

b) Focus on **message** of the word, not the fine particulars of a word, not the fine particulars of a word. Let **God** speak to you through the **message** of prophesy; not through the **dictionary**. Don't dissect your prophecy.

V. ESSENTIALS FOR FOLLOWING THROUGH ON INACCURATE AND/OR PRESUMPTUOUS WORDS

- Pastors and leaders must possess a proper attitude and perspective of prophetic ministry, and adjust their expectations. Not to expect or believe for the worse, but to prepare for such an occurrence (of an inaccurate or presumptuous prophecy) in their church which affects certain individuals, congregations, region(s), or nation(s).

- Proverbs 14:4 *"Where there is no ox, the stall is clean, but much increase comes from the strength of the ox."*

Just as it's impossible to have both a clean stall and the strength the ox gives, so it's impossible to enjoy the vital, life-giving flow of prophetic ministry without experiencing occasional problems. How problems are handled is the key. Here are some of the potential responses a pastor may have when confronted with a problem in the prophetic:

1) **Do nothing**: Failure to deal with it at all; ignore the misuse or abuse.

Result: Set the stage for abuse. Doing nothing about it implies that its okay and the problem will grow.

2) Shut down **prophetic** ministry altogether: After a negative experience, some may totally eliminate all expressions of spiritual gifts from their services.

Result: Neglecting to prophesy.

3) Shut down **individuals**: Label the person who made the mistake as false and forbid them from functioning, while allowing others to continue.

Result: No one will want to prophesy for fear of being labeled if they make a mistake.

4) **Control** and **encourage**: Properly discern, admit, correct and therefore learn from mistakes.
Result: Raise people up to the next level.

VI. A SPIRIT OF HUMILITY IS ESSENTIAL

- On behalf of the prophet which invites investigation and correction. Don't be self defensive and justify yourself or your ministry. God is our stronghold and he'll defend us.

- On behalf of the pastor showing genuine care for all concerned, and graciousness in handling any correction or restoration needed. Galatians 6:1

VII. RELATIONSHIP TO OTHER ELDERS

Maintain accountable relationships with a spiritual overseer and with other leaders in the body of Christ.

VIII. SCOPE OF MINISTRY

Proper follow-up to an inaccurate prophetic word will depend greatly on the time, place and setting in which the word was given.

1) If given in the local church, proper follow up should involve the local eldership, the prophet and those he relates to, and the person receiving the prophecy (if necessary).

2) If you gave an inaccurate word in a one-on-one setting, respond one-on-one, not in front of the whole church.

IX. USE OF PROPER MINISTERIAL ETHICS

- I Timothy 5:19 *"Receive not an accusation against an elder, except in the mouth of two or three."*

1) This is for the protection of leaders who could be slandered with false reports. Just as we should be careful not to receive an accusation against a man's morality or finances, we should also be careful not to slander a man's ministry by declaring he gave a false prophecy when facts do not absolutely substantiate it.

2) Even when substantiated, follow-up should always be handled by mature men who understand that God's purpose for discipline is redemptive and reconciliatory rather than punitive.

X. GIVE A BALANCED REPORT OF MINISTRY

If the inaccurate prophecy is dealt with publicly, it may provide a balanced perspective for the congregation to hear about all the accurate prophecies and quality ministry which took place in addition to the one inaccurate prophecy. This would keep some from developing an attitude of distrust toward a true prophet of God.

ADDITIONAL NOTES

PROPHETIC PITFALLS

God desires us to be faithful stewards and ministers of the gifts He has given to us. However, He is more interested in the character of the minister than in their ministry. With that in mind, the purpose of the Prophetic Pitfalls segment is to present teaching, using biblical examples of prophets and apostles, that will help you to 1) recognize root problems, character flaws and weed seed attitudes in your life that could hinder your ministry; 2) recognize common deceitful and destructive pitfalls and snares that could destroy your life and ministry.

The Prophet Elijah Pitfall of Discouragement and Pity 30
The Prophet Moses Pitfall of Overprotectiveness 36
Prophet Jonah's Pride and Judgment Pitfall 40
Prophet Balaam's Pitfall: True Prophesier but False Prophet........................45

THE PROPHET ELIJAH PITFALL:
Discouragement and Self-Pity

READ: I KINGS 17-19

I. ELIJAH - A MAN OF CONTRASTS

A. STRENGTHS

1) A man of prayer - he opened the heavens after a three year drought
2) A man of faith
3) A man of obedience to the voice of God
4) A man willing to put his life on the line to prove Jehovah was the true God - challenged 850 prophets of Baal

With such great strengths, one would think that he would be without character flaws & immune to satanic pitfalls but...

B. WEAKNESSES

1) Discouragement
2) Self-pity
3) "I alone am left syndrome" - I Kings 19:4

C. WHAT DO WE LEARN FROM ELIJAH'S WEAKNESSES?

1) I Kings 18:46; 19:1-3 - Everyone has a *button* that the devil can *push.*
2) I Kings 19:4 - When you *run* from something, you are headed for the *wilderness.*
3) Elijah portrays the prophet who is mighty in **prophesying** and in powerful **performance**, but weak in but weak in **personality**, attitude and adjustments to **rejection** and persecution.

II. DEATH WISH PRAYING

A. The plunge from the peak of powerful performances to the pit of self-pity and pessimistic death wish praying! - I Kings 19:4

Elijah confronts the prophets of Baal, yet one word from Queen Jezebel scares him bad enough to flee the land of Israel, run to the wilderness and sit under a juniper tree and pray that God would kill him.

B. "*I alone am left - no one understands me.*" Anytime you start thinking that way, you are headed for the **bottom** of the pit.

III. STAIR STEPS TO THE PIT

One reaches the pit of despair like descending a staircase. The first step is disappointment, and if not adjusted immediately with a proper attitude, then one will progressively begin the journey into the pit.

1) **Disappointment** - Disappointment can come from doing a great job and people do not show appreciation. Keep in mind that God will allow disappointment to develop your character. If you do not adjust immediately, a chain reaction starts to take place. Learn to adjust to offenses. Forgiveness is a process, not a gift of the Spirit. If you do not adjust your offenses, you will become disillusioned and disappointment will set in with yourself and others. This will take you to step #2 in your descent to the pit.

2) **Discouragement** - In discouragement, you lose your courage. You get your eyes on people and circumstances.

3) **Persecution complex** - This is the root of rejection. Unless you deal with the root, you cannot be saved from this complex. "*Poor me, nobody loves me, God and man are not doing right by me*" are the common symptoms. Best to believe that everyone loves you!

4) **Anger and Resentment** - Here you harbor your feelings and pinpoint enemies even to the point of being angry with God. You begin a conversation that is self-preserving in your heart.

5) **Bitter-Hard-Critical Spirit** - law unto themselves - A *spirit of error* comes before error!

a) How does it manifest itself? You begin to think, "Everybody missed it except ME! I am THE role model!"

b) If not checked, it will take a truth and make it a tragedy, a concept and make it a cult, a reality and make it bondage.

c) Those that step this far down the ladder usually develop the "sheriff" or "adjuster" attitude towards the Body of Christ. Their spirit becomes *judgmental* and they develop a judgmental spirit - Anytime someone becomes the authority for what is right or wrong, declaring what is doctrinally right, becoming dogmatic, narrow minded, and authoritarian, there is usually sin at the root. Something has gone wrong inside that individual's spirit. They usually fall into indiscretions of finances, drinking, immorality, or they will go off into cultic doctrine or heresy. Remember, God never made us to judge one another.

6) **Spirit of Rejection & Isolation**

a) In this step, you become a religious critic. No one around you is doing things right. You think, "*Everybody needs to hear my word.*" Remember, God has never limited Himself to a select few.

b Spirit of Rejection - Those with this spirit will do things subconsciously that they know will be rejected to prove to themselves that their self concepts are right. They will think, "*People do not like me, they are against me.*" Even when everything starts out well, they will set themselves up for rejection by producing positions, objectives, and limitations. They will say, "*If you really believe in me....*" or "*If you're going to stand with me, then you will do this and this...*" When these conditions are not fulfilled, they are then "rejected."

7) **Bottomless Pit of Self-Delusion** - In this stage, everybody else is wrong. You blame everyone and it is everybody else's fault that you are what you are and where you are.

8) **Restoration or Self-destruction** -
GET COMMITTED TO SOMEONE WHO CAN HELP YOU!

IV. CAVE MENTALITY - "I am the only one left!"

A. WEED SEED ATTITUDE OF SELF-PITY

Descending this prophetic pitfall staircase causes the man or women of God to develop a weed seed attitude of self-pity. Like Elijah, one may be caught thinking or saying such things as:

1) "Everybody is against me."
2) "Nobody understands my ministry."
3) "Nobody appreciates my great accomplishments or sacrifices."

B. SPIRIT OF ERROR

Those that make this mistake can remain pure in doctrine but they open themselves up to a spirit of error. They can develop the following tendencies:

1) an exclusive, seclusive spirit that forms a cult
2) a spirit that sows discord or suspicions
3) personal immorality
4) falling into a reprobate and backslidden condition

V. STEPS OUT OF THE CAVE MENTALITY

Isaiah 52:2 - "*Shake thyself from the dust...arise...loose thyself from the bands about thy neck.*"

REPENT & PROPERLY RESPOND!!

Get out of your self-pity party or your martyrdom-persecution complex. Adjust your wrong attitude and respond as if a rattlesnake had fallen on your head!

Only two things God will say in the cave:

1) "Prophet, what are you doing in here?" - You can go on a 10 day fast in the cave, but God says, "What are you doing here?"

2) "Get out of your cave and on the mountain before the Lord and listen for the voice of God!" – A new commission is given in I Kings 19:15-17.

"And the Lord said unto him, Go, return on thy way to the wilderness of Damascus: and when thou comest, anoint Hazael to be king over Syria: And Jehu the son of Nimshi shalt thou anoint to be king over Israel: and Elisha the son of Shaphat of Abelmeholah shalt thou anoint to be prophet in thy room. And it shall come to pass, that him that escapeth the sword of Hazael shall Jehu slay: and him that escapeth from the sword of Jehu, shall Elisha slay."

Get out of the cave and God will give you a ministry that will carry on after you're gone.

VI. RECEIVE EVERYTHING WITH GRACE

We must believe for grace to receive praise without becoming **proud** and receive persecution without developing a **persecution complex** and descending into the pit of **despair** and **self-delusion**.

ADDITIONAL NOTES

PROPHET MOSES' PITFALL: Overprotectiveness

Moses was a man who had to fulfill his role, not only as a father to a family, but also the role of a pastor to over three million of God's people. He carried the pastoral rod in his hand to shepherd and lead God's people from Egyptian bondage to freedom in the wilderness, and according to prophecy, he was to have taken them into the Promised Land.

Moses had a human virtue that became a vice--__________________________, when taken to the extreme, becomes a __________________________________

I. HUMAN COMPASSION AND MERCY VS. PROPHETIC PURPOSES AND GOD'S JUDGMENT

A. DILEMMA FOR PROPHETIC PASTORS

Like Moses, prophetic pastors can be torn between human mercy and compassion on the one hand, and God's judgment and prophetic purpose on the other.

B. MOSES' INTERCESSION WAS GOOD BUT...

Moses' intercession at the golden calf (Exodus 32:7-14) was admirable and a type of Christ at Calvary, but from God's perspective of His prophetic purpose, it was a hindrance. *Moses' root problem was* **overprotective** of his personal **pastoral** flock and too insistent that God had to **preserve** the established generation instead of **starting** afresh.

C. MOSES' WEAKNESS DISPLAYED NUMEROUS TIMES

"*Because all those men which have seen my glory, and my miracles, which I did in Egypt and in the wilderness, and have tempted me now these ten times, and have not hearkened to my voice.; Surely they shall not see the land which I sware unto their fathers......*" (Numbers 14:22-23)

Ten times the children of Israel provoked God's wrath while in the wilderness:

1) Exodus 14:11, 12 - accusing God of deceiving them and deliberately leading them into a trap so the Egyptians could kill them

2) Exodus 15:23-26 - murmuring at Marah for water

3) Exodus 16:1-8 - murmuring for flesh and bread before reaching Sinai

4) Exodus 16:19-22 - willful disobedience in leaving manna until morning

5) Exodus 17:1-7 - murmuring for water at Rephidim

6) Exodus 32 - making a golden calf and quickly going back to idolatry

7) Numbers 11:1-3 - murmuring at Taberah

8) Numbers 11 - murmuring for flesh

9) Numbers 13:1-25 with Deuteronomy 1:20-25 - unbelief in God and His words and asking that spies be sent into the land as if they doubted He told the truth

10) Numbers 13:26-14:37, Deuteronomy 1:20-25 - rebellion at Kadesh

God repeatedly told Moses that his congregation was full of stiff-necked, self-willed saints who belonged to the "old order." (They had come out of Egypt but Egypt wasn't out of them!) Several times God wanted to kill off the "older generation," but Moses argued with God and insisted that He must preserve them.

D. END RESULT OF OVERPROTECTIVENESS

The old murmuring Israelites finally pushed Moses beyond his patience, so that he angrily struck the rock instead of speaking to it according to God's prophetic instructions (Exodus 20:7-13). Thus, his act of impatience, frustration, self-will, and disobedience cancelled that part of his personal prophecy which said he would go into Canaan.

II. LESSONS LEARNED FROM MOSES

Three lessons (biblical truths) can be learned from this incident:

1) Our **actions** can cancel part of our **personal prophecy**.
Even after much that has been prophesied about us is fulfilled, our actions can cancel prophecies that remain unfulfilled. Our remaining unfulfilled prophecies will be fulfilled depending upon our *continual faith, obedience and patience.*

2) God's grace for **endurance** doesn't extend beyond the bounds of God's **purpose**.

Like Moses, when we demand that God do things our own way, then we are on our own. God might very well just give us what we want - to our own destruction.
The following examples illustrate this point:

- Israelites grumbling about manna - They craved meat, so God sent quail - but even as they ate the meat, a severe plague broke out and killed many (see Numbers 11).
- King Hezekiah of Israel - When God prophetically decreed through Isaiah that he would die, the king wept bitterly and begged for an extension of life (Isaiah 38). In response, God granted 15 more years, but in those added years, Hezekiah's behavior led to disaster for the nation! He and the people would have been better off if the original prophetic decrees had been fulfilled as it led to the death of his family and captivity for all Israel.
- Prodigal son (Luke 15) - The son demands his inheritance before the proper timing and the Father allows him to waste it all and go into ruin.
- Apostle Paul reveals in the New Testament that those who hate truth and insist on harboring falsehood get what they want in the end, to their own doom. He said of them, "*They perish because they refused to love the truth and so be saved. For this reason God sent them a powerful delusion so that they would believe the lie and so that all would be condemned who had not believed the truth but had delighted in wickedness* " (2 Thessalonians 2:10,11 NIV)

3) *Pastoral compassion and prophetic purpose will sometimes be at odds.* Many times, this struggle will cause friction and even conflict within the local church between the pastor and prophet. The key to maintaining unity is to seek God with a humble heart.

   Moses' insistence and compassion was commendable from a pastoral perspective, but from a prophetic perspective, his actions were foolish and futile. (Remember, God still had to kill off almost the entire older generation to see His purposes fulfilled.)

4) Pastors today must not be **overprotective**.
   Don't insist that old wineskin saints or a denomination has to come in... If so, you may die in the wilderness with them. When prophet shepherds are overprotective of their flocks, (so mercy motivated that they will not allow God to chasten properly those under their charge) they set themselves up for the Moses pitfall.

III. GOD'S PROPHETIC PURPOSE IS GREATER THAN HUMAN PREFERENCE

It makes no difference to God what man's reputation or stature is - whether they give ten thousand dollars or be a founding member of the church. Those in leadership must follow God's directives! They owe no allegiance to man and should feel no obligation to the "old order" portion of their congregation. If they do, they will never enter into present truth or fulfill their prophetic potential.

PROPHET JONAH'S PITFALLS: Pride and Judgment

Jonah had the weed seed attitude of pride and a root problem of being to **judgemental_** (see Jonah 1-4). While Moses' weakness was too much mercy, Jonah was motivated too much by judgment. He was more interested in seeing God destroy the wicked than having mercy upon them. He had the character flaw of being more **concerned** with his reputation than with the people he **ministered too**.

I. THE RESENTFUL ANGRY PROPHET SYNDROME

A. BASED UPON A ROOT SYSTEM

Some grieve more over the loss of their "gourd shade" of personal comfort than they do over the death of thousands of people. Their resentment can be traced to the root system of:

selfishness	pride
anger	vengeance
self-will	personal ambition

Because of this, they run from any spiritual assignment which has the possibility of making them look bad or failing to bring them a profit.

Sometimes you need to forgive God in order to release yourself from your judgment. You also need to forgive anyone else so that they can be released from your judgment. Remember, if someone has treated you unfairly, **rejoice** because it is a part of God's course of training!

How can one change? God sometimes must providentially force the individual to be His spokesman by putting them into a restrictive situation at the bottom of the ocean of life until they are willing to obey.

B. GOD HAS A RIGHT TO CHANGE HIS MIND

God's heart is more for people to change than to see His judgment go unchanged.

II. IMMATURE PROPHETS WHO RESPOND TO GOD LIKE SPOILED CHILDREN

- How do they respond to God?

1) Like spoiled children, they **dictate** to God how His word should be **fulfilled** because they do **not** trust God to do it the way they think it should be **done**.

2) They try to threaten and intimidate God by saying such things as, "*God, if you don't treat me better, I won't be your spokesman.*" Or they might say, "*I'll run away, backslide, quit the ministry [or a dozen other childish things] if you don't do it my way! If I do that for you, you must do this for me. You owe me, God! This isn't fair, I deserve better than this*!"

The Lord will never go against your will but as a Father, He knows how to make you very willing. [Jesus Boat vs. Jonah Boat - Remember, the storm does not determine the will of God; it is whether you have Jesus on board or whether you are going away from Him.]

III. ANGER AND RESENTMENT AT GOD'S DEALINGS

- *Points to ponder*:

1) Prophetic people must beware of the Jonah pitfall. You must not develop an angry bitter spirit towards God because of His severe dealings and His perfecting processes.

2) When you become angry at God, the devil doesn't have to come near you. You become so wrapped up in yourself that he doesn't have to come near to keep you from being effective for God.

3) Realize that you do not have any enemies in the world. They are all your friends and teachers! (Romans 8:31-39) If God be for you, who can be against you? Your enemies do nothing but force you into the mold of Jesus Christ.

4) Everything that God causes to happen to you is designed to fulfill God's greater purpose!

5) Anger and a pessimistic attitude will cost you! We have no record that Jonah was ever used by God again.

___

___

___

___

IV. BE ADJUSTABLE AND CORRECTABLE

- Don't try to justify your attitude or action. Remember that every weed seed attitude and every sin has its own justifications (arguments as to why they are justified to be the way they are.)

- Place yourself in an arena of true biblical accountability and allow others to tell you the truth about yourself.

  "Faithful are the wounds of a friend; but the kisses of an enemy are deceitful." (Proverbs 27:6)

- If everyone you associate with always tells you how great you are, then watch out! This means that you don't have faithful sailors who are willing to throw you overboard into God's purpose for your life.

  "Woe unto you, when all men shall speak well of you! For so did their fathers to the false prophets." (Luke 6:26)

ADDITIONAL NOTES

PROPHET BALAAM'S PITFALL:
True Prophesier but False Prophet

The prophet Balaam should be studied thoroughly by every person who feels called to the prophetic office (see Numbers 22:1-24; 25; 31:8-16; Deuteronomy 23:5, 6; Joshua 13:22, 24; 9, 10; Micah 6:5; Hebrews 2:15; Jude 11; Revelation 2:14). Balaam could give a true word, yet he became a false prophet in his personal attitude and life. His example should teach us that judging the prophet and judging the prophetic word are two different matters.

I. PRINCIPLES FOR JUDGING FALSE PROPHECY VS. A FALSE PROPHET

A. PROPHECY JUDGED IN THREE AREAS:

The spiritual message must conform to biblical truth - not to witness with your doctrine but with the Word of God and your spirit.

Objective, verifiable statements about the past and present can be checked against the facts.... but remember that our perspective of things, even the facts, can sometimes be improperly perceived.

Predictions about the future are judged by whether they come to pass. Again, we must remember that prophecy is conditional even when conditions are not put on it (see *Prophets and Personal Prophecy, Volume #1* - pgs. 145-154).

B. PROPHETS JUDGED DIFFERENTLY THAN PROPHECY

True and false prophetic ministers are discerned by:

- Their **character**.
- Their **spirit of wisdom** (James 3:13-18). Earthly wisdom is self-seeking, God's wisdom is God seeking and God promoting.
- The **fruit of the Holy Spirit** in their personal lives (Galatians 5:22).
- The **fruit of their ministry** that remains after the initial manifestations of miracles or other signs.

II. O.T. PORTRAYAL OF BALAAM VS. N.T. DECLARATION AND DESCRIPTION OF BALAAM

A. OLD TESTAMENT

As we read the Old Testament, we see that Balaam held to one important prophetic rule: He refused to prophesy anything except what God had given him to say. Seemingly, his ministry and his methods look true until one investigates what the New Testament conveys about him.

B. NEW TESTAMENT

Reading passages in the New Testament, one sees that Balaam is judged a false prophet by:

- **Jesus** - "*But I have a few things against thee, because thou hast there them that hold the doctrine of Balaam, who taught Balac to cast a stumbling block before the children of Israel, to eat things sacrificed unto idols, and to commit fornication.*" (Revelation 2:14)

- **Peter** - "*Which have forsaken the right way, and are gone astray, following the way of Balaam the son of Bosor, who loved the wages of unrighteousness; But was rebuked for his iniquity: the dumb ass speaking with man's voice forbad the madness of the prophet.*" (2 Peter 2:15, 16)

- **Jude** - "*Woe unto them! for they have gone in the way of Cain, and ran greedily after error of Balaam for reward, and perished in the gainsaying of Core.*" (Jude 11)

III. M'S OF MESSAGE, MINISTRY, MANHOOD VS. MOTIVE, MATURITY, METHODS, AND MONEY

In the Old Testament, Balaam's message, ministry, manhood and morality appear to be in order, but the New Testament reveals that his "M's" of motive, maturity, methods, and money were not.

- **Balaam lusted for possessions and power** (Jude 11).

  God told Balaam when he first inquired that he was not to go with Balak to curse Israel. After further offers of reward, however, Balaam inquired of God again to see if there was not some way he could go. Yet there is no indication in the scriptural text that this confirmation came before Balaam saddled up his donkey to go to Balak to prophesy against Israel.

- **Balaam's counsel caused the children of Israel to trespass against the Lord**. (Numbers 31:7-16)

- **Balaam's prophetic message was accurate but his way, (course of life), was in error.** Numbers 22:32 states, "*And the Angel of the LORD said to him, 'Why have you struck your donkey these three times? Behold, I have come out to stand against you, because your way is perverse before me.'*"

Psalm 37:23 states, "*The steps of a good man are ordered of the LORD, and He delights in his way.*"

IV. POINTS TO PONDER ABOUT BALAAM

A. HOW MANY M's CAN BE OUT OF ORDER BEFORE BEING A FALSE PROPHET?

Sometimes ONLY ONE!

B. A SELF-WILLED PROPHET TAKES A MILE WHEN GOD GIVES AN INCH

God was angry with Balaam because even after telling him not to go with Balak, Balaam persisted. God sent an angel to cause a breakdown in Balaam's transportation so that he would be stopped.

C. EVEN A DONKEY CAN DISCERN BETTER THAN A PROPHET BLINDED BY LUST FOR RICHES, POWER AND PROMOTION

A blinded prophet is dumber than a donkey! The donkey saw God's providential restriction, but the prophet Balaam was too blinded by his self-will to see that God was involved in frustrating his situation.

D. BALAAM WANTED TO PLEASE PEOPLE FOR POSITION

Balaam's potential for the rewards of riches, influenced him to displease God and strive to please people for earthly gain. His ROOT PROBLEM – **"love of money"** (I Timothy 6:10). He tried to serve God and Mammon at the same time.

[**NOTE**: Balaam could have held a secret resentment in his heart toward Jehovah for not allowing him to prophesy anything that Balak desired against Israel - thus causing him to lose all of Balak's promised riches and promotion. Balaam could not prophesy anything except what God told him, but he finally by-passed that restriction by not prophesying in the name of Jehovah. Instead, he pulled upon his prophetic insight and gave counsel to the Moabites and Midianites about how they could destroy the Israelites by causing them to sin against God by adultery and idolatry (Revelation 2:14). By doing so, Balaam finally received the riches and position he wanted, but he was also destroyed with the Midianites under the judgment of God (Joshua 13:22).]

____

____

____

____

____

____

V. SEEING PROPHETS AS GOD SEES THEM

A. FROM MAN'S PERSPECTIVE

Reading about Balaam in the book of Numbers, he seemingly does not look false or wrongly motivated. Again, only in light of the New Testament (Peter's, Jude's and Jesus' comments) do we begin to see Balaam like God saw him. If we were to judge this prophet only by the accuracy of his prophecies, we would have to declare him a true prophet.

Balaam prophesied only what God spoke to him even though he was offered great riches. The references in Numbers make him look like a man of integrity in the prophetic ministry who resisted all temptations. In fact, he gives the only Messianic prophecy in the book of Numbers, and he was the greatest prophet among his peers.

B. FROM GOD'S PERSPECTIVE

Balaam's false status is only perceived by God's spirit of discernment which searches the heart and the motive. The scriptures declare that man looks on the outward appearance, but God weighs the spirit and identifies the motive behind the performance.

"*But the Lord said unto Samuel, Look not on his countenance, or on the height of his stature; because I have refused him: for the Lord seeth not as man seeth; for man looketh on the outward appearance, but the Lord looketh on the heart.*" (1 Samuel 16:7)

> "*All the ways of a man are clean in his own eyes; but the Lord weigheth the spirits.*" (Proverbs 16:2)

____
____
____
____
____
____
____
____

VI. MOTIVE PLUS ACTION EQUALS DEED (M + A = D)

A. BOOK OF REVELATION

The book of Revelation says that every person's eternal reward and destiny will be determined by his or her deeds. Deeds are more than actions; they are formed by two factors: MOTIVE AND ACTIONS. So when God judges someone to be true or false, He not only perceives their actions, but the motive behind the actions.

B. WOLVES IN SHEEP'S CLOTHING

"*Beware of false prophets which come to you in sheep's clothing, but inwardly they are ravening wolves. Ye shall know them by their fruits.....Not everyone that saith unto me, Lord, Lord, shall enter into the kingdom of heaven: but he that doeth the will of my Father which is in heaven. Many will say to me in that day, Lord, Lord, have we not prophesied in thy name? and in thy name have cast out devils? and in thy name done many wonderful works? And then I will profess unto them, I never knew you: depart from me, ye that work iniquity.*" (Matthew 7:15, 16, 21-23)

Jesus said prophets and saints can have the outward appearance and ministry of a sheep but the inward spirit and motivation of a wolf. These represent prophets and prophetic people with accurate prophecies and miraculous works, but they are not righteous - not right inside.

C. FALSE PROPHET GIVING A TRUE WORD VS. TRUE PROPHET GIVING FALSE PROPHECY

Scripture records a number of individuals who gave false words and are later evaluated and judged as false prophets. But Balaam is the only one who portrays the reality that a prophet can give accurate prophecies and yet be a wrong enough person on the inside to be judged a false prophet.

Most Christians know Deuteronomy 18:22 that declares a person's "true prophet" status is determined by whether the word that person gives is accurate and comes to pass. But again, we must remember that Prophet Balaam only spoke God-directed words, and they came to pass....but the New Testament uses him as an example of what a prophet should not be and do.

God is more concerned about the purity of His prophets than the accuracy of their prophecies! He values the men and women themselves and their motives as well as their message and ministry!

Also, Deuteronomy 13:1-3 confirms that a person can prophesy accurately, yet be false by leading people astray and away from the Lord.

> *"If there arise among you a prophet, or a dreamer of dreams, and giveth thee a sign or a wonder, And the sign or the wonder come to pass, whereof he spake unto thee, saying, Let us go after other gods, which thou hast not known, and let us serve them; Thou shalt not hearken unto the words of that prophet, or that dreamer of dreams: for the Lord your God proveth you, to know whether ye love the Lord your God with all your heart and with all your soul."*

[For more information, please read pgs. 124-138 in *Prophets, Pitfalls and Principles, Volume #3* by Dr. Hamon]

VII. INTIMACY WITH GOD

Remember, Jesus will say to some, "Depart from me ye workers of iniquity, I never knew you." The verb "to know" is used in the Hebrew of the Old Testament to convey the intimate relationship between husband and wife... as in "Adam knew his wife Eve" (Genesis 4:1). Similarly, Jesus uses the word "knew" in the above passage to convey that some prophets will have at one time gone through the "legal ceremony" of being born-again. They will use their God-given gifts and talents to prophesy and do wondrous miracles but in the end, they never allowed Jesus' life and motive to become their motivation and purpose for ministry. So in that day, Jesus will say to them, that He never knew them.

A. WE MUST GUARD AGAINST SELF-DECEPTION, WRONG MOTIVE, AND SELF JUSTIFICATION

Proverbs 16:2 states: "*all the ways of a man are clean in his own eyes...*"

And Jeremiah the prophet stated, "*The heart is deceitful above all things, and desperately wicked; who can know it*?" (Jeremiah 17:9)

B. WE NEED ACCOUNTABILITY TO APOSTOLIC AND PROPHETIC FATHERS

We all have blind spots. For this reason, every saint and minister needs to submit to someone he or she respects enough to listen to provides instruction and correction.

⇨ **STUDENT:**

1) Ask God to deliver you from the Balaam motivation.
2) Find someone who can discern your spirit, is willing to tell you what they see, and can help deliver you from the error of Balaam.

ADDITIONAL NOTES

ACTIVATIONS

To *activate* is to stir up the gifts of the spirit within, or make them become active. We are exhorted in 1 Peter 4:10, "As each one has received a gift, minister it to one another, as good stewards of the manifold grace of God." The activation portion of this module gives you a *safe place* to exercise your faith in manifesting spiritual gifts. Because it is just practice, you have an opportunity to overcome any fears in moving in spiritual gifts.

Activations Overview 54
Activation Guidelines 56

BRIEF OVERVIEW OF ACTIVATIONS

I. EXPLANATION OF ACTIVATIONS

What does "activation" mean? Why do we activate? How does it work?

A. Definition*:* We are going to set up a situation where we will ask you to hear from God, and then communicate what you get from God, under these conditions:

1. Do it the way we ask you to do it.
2. Give permission for others in the room to make a mistake, including yourself.

EXHORTATION:

Students, remember that fear brings a snare. It controls you by keeping you from doing what you are supposed to do. Fear is anti-faith. Fear kills faith because you don't act. Faith is doing something. Activating is acting. Step past your fears. Remember, God has given you a **spirit of power, love, and a sound mind!**

B. Why do we activate?

1. Sports analogy: When you want to be excellent in sports, you train. While you train, you may do things that have nothing to do with the actual sport you are training for. For example, swimmers do weight training; boxers run in training; runners do sit-ups. These types of things develop strength, flexibility, and endurance. When athletes are actually in competition, the activities they performed in training will be put to use. It's the same with activations. We are training you to hear God's voice in a safe atmosphere, so that when the "real life" situations arise, you will have more confidence and ability.

2. When we are doing activations, we are in the gym, speaking metaphorically. We will ask you to do things. When you are in training, there are no mistakes. The only way you can fail in training is by not training! You will find your limits and break through them. For example, you may be asked to prophesy to someone you don't

know, someone you can't see, for a short time, for a long time, behind someone, or in front of someone.

C. Rules

1. Don't take a word you receive in training and treat it the same as you would in the competition. Go for it and mess up! Mistakes are okay. No one is perfect when they start.
2. The gifts are developed by reason of use. Press through barriers.
3. We are stewards of the gifts He has given. Don't bury your gift. Take a risk.

II. KEY POINTS/FEEDBACK

After the activation, you may have related to some of the following key points:

- You heard a phrase, or saw a picture. It's like a Polaroid camera. Let God develop it. Don't make it develop or try to interpret it yourself.
- It's okay if what you received was not specific. It may seem vague to you, but very specific to the person receiving the word.
- It may not make sense to you, but perfect sense to the person receiving the word.
- God knows what the receiver needs. If you get something very general, like "God loves you" or "He is well pleased with you", give it anyway. It may be a rhema to the receiver, and exactly what they needed at that time.
- Person may not relate to the word at that time. It may have been something in the past that they had forgotten about or something they may relate to in the future.
- Person may relate to some of the word, but not all of it. Don't throw the baby out with the bath water. Put what you don't understand on the shelf.

III. ACTIVATION GUIDELINES

1. There is a special time and place to be activated. Don't do it elsewhere without proper oversight.

2. Don't make any major decisions on a prophetic word you receive in an activation time. Allow God to confirm it independently by established ministers and wise counsel.

3. Write out your word as soon as possible. Keep it in a notebook with the rest of your prophecies.

4. Counsel with your pastor/elder about all words you receive.

5. Seek to edify the Body when ministering spiritual gifts.

6. Be teachable.

7. Flow with the order of the service.

8. Give personal words only under pastoral supervision.

Made in the USA
Middletown, DE
27 April 2023

29510980R00035